Maaya Rodriques

Journey to Hephzibah

Arise and Claim Your Name

ISBN:

Paperback: 978-976-97081-9-8

Editor: Bloomin Daily Publishers

First Edition 2024.

Table of Contents

Introduction 1

Chapter 1: Rebellion 3

Chapter 2: Asleep at the Bosom of God 12

Chapter 3: Spiritual and Physical Losses 15

Chapter 4: Open the Eyes of The Blind 21

Chapter 5: Deliverance in Jesus' Name 30

Chapter 6: Revelations 37

Chapter 7: A New Name - Hephzibah 44

Glossary 54

About The Author 59

Introduction

For as the earth bringeth forth her bud, and as the garden causeth the things that are sown in it to spring forth; so the Lord GOD will cause righteousness and praise to spring forth before all the nations.

Isaiah 61:11 KJV

It was in 2009 that the transformation of my life began. It was at Moorelands camp, a Christian retreat nestled in the hills of Trelawny, that I received a prophecy that not only provided insight into my life but also gave me a glimpse into the future. That defining moment impacted my life and made me who I am today.

A lady prophesied that she saw me in a desert and I was like a dry flower. I was stunned, bewildered, and dissatisfied all at the same time as I could not understand why she had likened me to a desert and a dry flower. During this time, my connection with the Lord was strained. I was curious about who God is but I didn't understand the words written in the Bible, I didn't know what His voice was like, or what to expect from my journey with the Lord.

A few years later however, the Lord led me to **Isaiah 61:11**. After reading this scripture, my thoughts rushed back to the prophecy and I reflected on how God had lavishly watered my life. But, it wasn't before I had gone through several years of pain. How desolate I had been, just like the desert. How, like a flower, I was given everything I needed to grow, but I couldn't because of my surroundings.

This book is dedicated to everyone who feels like a dried flower, your day will come to be watered. You will bloom.

CHAPTER 1

Rebellion

*Honour your father and your mother, that your days may
be long in the land that the Lord your God is giving you.*

Exodus 20:12 KJV

*Suppose one of you has a hundred sheep and loses one of
them. Doesn't he leave the ninety-nine in the open country
and go after the lost sheep until he finds it and goes
home? Then he calls his friends and neighbours together
and says, Rejoice with me; I have found my lost sheep.*

Luke 15:4-6 KJV

*In a dream, in a vision of the night, When deep sleep
falleth upon men, In slumberings upon the bed; Then he
openeth the ears of men, And sealeth their instruction,
That he may withdraw man from his purpose, And hide
pride from man. He keepeth back his soul from the pit,
And his life from perishing by the sword.*

Job 33:15-18 KJV

A fter graduating high school, I was determined to forge my own path in life. I opted to study cosmetology as it was a stepping stone to becoming a trichologist. I believed that my love for hair knew no bounds and I wanted to help people grow their hair with love.

Even though I had career goals, my thoughts were consumed with what I considered to be the highlights of life as a teenager. I would dream of sharing an amazing apartment with my best friend, Paige. Travelling around Jamaica, going to parties, and having boyfriends while finding our place and way in life. And boy, did I find it.

Shortly after being enrolled in beauty school I encountered a guy, Scan, who had a selfish agenda. He was a prominent lawyer during the day and a budding artiste during his free time. I remember seeing an advertisement of his - he wanted dancers for a music video. I decided to call the number and express my interest. I can remember him making sexual overtures towards me as soon as I met him in person. Seeing I was new to having an older guy display interest towards me, I entertained him and soon found myself between a rock and a hard place.

There were days when we met to talk in his car at a public space and he made sexual advances towards me. I always found a way to deny him by saying I was not ready or I was nervous. I quickly realised he was becoming impatient and demanding with my time, so I decided it was best to stay away. I remember feeling anxious and pressured every time he thought he had the right to kiss and touch me. It made me feel awful. He had a lustful spirit, and I was too naive to handle the situation.

One Friday, in July 2012, I decided not to see him again and called him the following day to tell him I would not be having sex with him. After that refusal, he verbally harassed me everyday or every other day straight until 2017. He called me saying nasty, perverted things that made me so worried. I used to glance out my window to see if he was there based on what he said. It was frightening.

My parents noticed a change in my behaviour, I was impatient, worried, depressed and paranoid. I didn't know what to do or what to say to the people who were concerned. At one point, my mom asked me again, for the umpteenth time if I was okay, and I burst into tears and finally spoke some of the truth. I was too afraid to let my mom know the extent of the harassment and how hurt I was. My mom must have sensed much of what I wasn't telling her, she instructed me to ignore him and recommended that I get a medical check-up. Unfortunately, I refused.

I used to think my family overprotected me and I longed to experience life the way I thought other children my age did. They were free to go on social outings or partying - whilst my parents were unwilling to send me anywhere. And so, despite what I faced with Sean, the rebellious side of me always went exploring.

One summer a friend of mine, Peter, introduced me to a martial art form called Capoeira. He had just started and would frequently meet with his training partners to drill or perfect his talents. I was fascinated. I wanted to learn how to defend myself against perverts like Sean. I asked Paige if she wanted to try out Capoeira with me. She agreed, so we approached our parents for permission which they gave. With that, we arranged to meet Peter at Emancipation Park for our first class. Paige and I were excited when we saw the guys we were going to practise with. We had never seen so many guys working out in one place before. Shortly after, Paige and I became attracted to the lead student, Nate. Paige however, had a boyfriend so I felt free to pursue Nate. I had assumed she wouldn't have been too upset, but my interest in Nate soon put a strain on our friendship.

During our training, I found Nate to be quite intriguing. I was always amazed at how talented he was while practising Capoeira. He knew how to captivate an audience and persuade people to do what he wanted.

One evening after training I asked him where he was from and he told me he was born in Jamaica and lived with his mom, brother and nieces. He told me about his mom's business and how she always struggled to provide for them even when she didn't have it to give. When I asked about his dad, he told me he didn't have a relationship with him because of his decision to abandon him and his other siblings. Nate's siblings blamed their mother for having another child, Nate, with a man who was so reckless. They also hated Nate, because they were stuck taking care of him much of the time. To make matters worse, the only sibling that cared for Nate was killed one night by his own friends. Because of all this Nate was bitter, filled with rage, loneliness, and unforgiveness.

When he shared details of his upbringing with me, I realised that his past had led him to develop a negative outlook on the world. He believed life was cruel to people who lived in the inner cities. I sympathised with him and knew I wanted to know more. I believed beneath all that hate and pain, there was good in store for Nate, and I could be the one that brought healing into his life. I wanted to share God's word with him and also that there were good people in the world too. I tried to show him this by sharing the good experiences I had in life. After all, my brother and I grew up in a loving, Christ- filled environment where we were protected spiritually and physically. Whenever I spoke, Nate always said I didn't know what I was talking about. It seemed as if Nate wanted to grow his fury about how the world operated in terms of the economy and social class instead of making peace with it. He felt the world owed him everything, so he liked to use his intelligence and manipulation to get what he wanted.

On one of our dates, Nate explained to me that he got into bad company because of his mother's lack of responsibility. She was always so busy trying to make ends meet that she could not watch out for him.

He shared how a man approached him looking for young talent for an advertisement. While working on the advertisement, the man offered him a place to stay. There, he was introduced to books about witchcraft, reiki and demonology. He often saw demons walking across his room or smelled strange things. He shared that through his new found knowledge he was able to heal himself and read people like a book. He could tell a stranger their name or something unique about themselves. Whenever he demonstrated this skill, people were always blown away. And so was I, so I followed Nate and practised Capoeira with him.

Few people are aware of this style of martial arts. It began among slaves in Portugal and Brazil. It was often practised by marginalised communities and used as a means to resist oppression.

The art incorporates dance, acrobatics, music, and spirituality. But, the untold secret in Capoeira is the witchcraft at play. Some capoeira practitioners believed in the power of spiritual elements and incorporated rituals and spells into their training. While not all knowingly engage in witchcraft, the connection between capoeira and witchcraft adds an intriguing and mystical element to its already rich history and cultural significance.

Capoeira looks like a beautiful performance in the eyes of the beholder but with a spiritual eye, you can see the dangers of idolatry and witchcraft coming into play. Each game encourages the spirit of deception which is called mandinga. To play the game, each participant needs to create a roda, which is a circle. The Contra Mestre or leader sits at the head, and then persons take turns playing instruments such as the berimbau. This traditional instrument is used to accompany the claps and chants of songs such as Modela, Boa Noite, A Hora É Essa, Paranauê Paraná, and Quem Vem Lá. These were only a few of the numerous songs they had. All of this was happening to set the atmosphere while both players took their place at the centre of the roda. The players moved in time with the tune or how fast or slow the claps are.

After a while of training with these folks at Emancipation Park, they encouraged me to formally train with them. While playing with the moves I was taught, I always felt something inside of me- it had the ability to shift your mood - often encouraging malicious intents, deception, or anger. At this point in my life, I was operating on an auto pilot. There was something wrong but I couldn't put a finger on it and Capoeira had me completely absorbed.

Even with my family's conviction that it was a cult and God revealing to me through dreams that I experienced a change in my spirit each time I engaged in Capoeira I didn't behave in any way that suggested I was trying to flee. I was so engrossed with Nate and the art of self-defence that I did not see that my ship was sinking. And it wouldn't be until a few months later that I would begin to see the signs.

Some time after, I entered a competition and was awarded an intern position as a junior editor at a prominent newspaper. My focus had changed from trichology and I was now leaning towards public relations and journalism. After my internship, I was accepted to the University of the West Indies and I could only see an amazing future. But my excitement quickly dimmed when just a few months after attending classes I found out that Nate and I were expecting.

I confided in my older cousin Ana, that I was pregnant and too scared to tell my parents. Ana offered to share the news. She told my dad and they both shared the news with my mom. My parents were deeply hurt that I was pregnant for a man I was not married to. Their disappointment in me plus the fact that my studies were now challenged was hard to bear. On top of that, my mom confided in my best friend's mom about the matter, and instead of offering support, she withdrew and disassociated herself from the situation.

My rebellion had led to so much pain, regrets, and disappointments, and this was just the beginning.

CHAPTER 2

Asleep at the Bosom of God.

Behold, all his fellows shall be ashamed: and the workmen, they are of men: let them all be gathered together, let them stand up; yet they shall fear, and they shall be ashamed together.

Isaiah 44:11 KJV

Shortly after breaking the news that I was pregnant I began spending more time with Nate because I was feeling unwelcome in my own home. Nate and I had a toxic relationship; he didn't know what he wanted out of the relationship and I didn't respect myself enough to leave for good. We were good one minute, then he'd believe we were not a good match or that something didn't seem quite right. I'd leave him, quite distraught and like a yo-yo, returned to him whenever he discovered I wasn't there for him. I just kept telling myself it would work out and comforted him by reassuring him that he was loved and not the broken person he believed himself to be.

But, how could one love and expect love from someone who believed they were unworthy of love?

Now, when I first told Nate of my pregnancy, he did not handle it well. It seemed no one, except Nate's mother, was happy. This was a heartbreaking process, and at first, I believed it would be better for everyone if the baby didn't exist. But, regardless of what anyone thought, my love for my baby grew as she grew.

I remember having a dream in which the Contra Mestre told me my baby was unwell, and I responded, "okay", whilst pondering why he was telling me this. I got up from the dream that morning without rebuking it, a big mistake. At the clinic a week later I asked the nurse if I could have my child delivered early, and she said she couldn't unless something was wrong. I was upset, but I did not make a fuss. The doctor told me to return to the clinic in two weeks instead of a week, which I considered odd given that I was thirty-five weeks pregnant and nearing the end of my pregnancy.

The day I became thirty-seven weeks I began to feel strange, I was sweating and experiencing something that felt like braxton hicks contractions. Upon learning that I was not well, my mom suggested that Nate take me to the hospital. She expressed that she had a dream of me dressed in white with flames surrounding me. My stomach was flat and I was saying, "the baby, the baby!"

I informed Nate that I was not feeling well and I needed to go to the hospital, but he refused because he did not see the need. My mom was unable to transport me to the hospital because she did not know my exact address. Nate was ashamed of where we lived so he had asked me not to disclose his address to my parents. I felt hopeless.

To this day I am grateful to God for how he held my family together throughout this ordeal of shame and hurt. Despite the challenges we encountered God gave my parents oil, knowledge and comfort. Because, even at this point, even though I had given my life to Jesus through baptism I wasn't able to really soak in the messages God wanted to share with me. I remained stubborn and dedicated to pleasing the idols I had in my life, my boyfriend and the art of Capoeira. But, looking back at this moment with fresh revelation from God, even though I had turned my back on God, He still had me in His bosom. Because he alone would have been able to get me through what would happen next.

CHAPTER 3
Spiritual and Physical Losses

The grass withereth, the flower fadeth: but the word of our God shall stand for ever.

Isaiah 40:8 KJV

Don't worry, Ci-Ana, you have me," I told my unborn child. " I'll take care of you baby girl," I pledged. One week after I made this pledge, I went for my regular check-up at the clinic and we discovered that my baby girl, Ci-Ana, was thirty-eight weeks old and had no heartbeat. I was hurt, and felt like Nate, my parents, and my relatives had gotten what they wanted. She was gone in an instant.

Later that night I was admitted to the hospital so that they could prepare for Ci-Ana's birth. I thought it was unfair and painful to give birth to my baby. My bed in the hospital was by a window and I often peered out the window with grief in my heart and questions running through my mind. How and why did this occur? Was it my fault that she died? Was it because her father's blood and mine were not compatible? We had done several ultrasounds during this pregnancy and everything seemed fine, so I was bewildered by what happened.

In retrospect, I think I asked all these questions because I did not remember the dream I had of the Contra Mestre telling me the baby was sick and that I did not condemn the dream, so the dream legally proceeded. Throughout the pregnancy, Nate also had dreams about Ci-Ana. In these dreams she was wrapped in cloth and looked dark. He had those nightmares all the time, but he didn't believe in rebuking dreams, and therefore, the unfortunate happened.

After Ci-Ana's birth, on March 19, 2015, the nurse allowed her father and me to spend some time with her. She surprised me with her attractiveness: clearly delineated lips, a dimpled chin, and a round face inherited from my mother.

I changed my mind about having the physicians perform an autopsy on my baby girl's body because her body was still perfect. No matter how lifeless it was, I didn't want anybody else touching her besides my family. I recall watching my brother cry, my mom was there for support, and my dad was there from a distance. I believe he was hurt and coped with it from a distance. My aunts were in anguish, but they stood by me, providing literature and comfort.

When the undertakers came to collect her body, we were still at the hospital. Witnessing their arrival brought on another wave of pain. We opted to have her cremated rather than hold a family funeral service - I wouldn't have had much to say at her funeral other than how lovely she was, that she moved to the sound of her father's voice and seemed to love us as much as we did her. I often wondered, before she was born into heaven, if she'd be as feisty as I was with my mother, but I never found out. We made cute necklaces and a blue striped gold urn for her ashes, which I stored for years before ultimately releasing them. Nate lost the pendant we got with Ci-Ana's remains one day during his workout - he was often misplacing or losing items. It didn't sit well with me.

Nate and I became pregnant again shortly after Cici's death, this time with twins! Surprise! I was astounded, as were my family members, but we were overjoyed, hopeful, cautious, and anxious to have these two bundles of joy in our arms.

Nate experienced visions of the twins being dust, dark, and not alive shortly after our pregnancy. The one dream we had in common was realising they were twins before the ultrasound confirmed it. I constantly told Nate that nothing bad would happen to these babies, that I would be more cautious and relaxed. By this time, we had gotten married, and I had hoped that the marriage would make things better. Perhaps marriage would lessen the disappointment or consequences of having our first child outside of marriage. I believed being spiritually ignorant of God's Word - not knowing the whole meaning of marriage and what it meant spiritually - had significant consequences. And we wanted everything to be perfect. This time we even chose to deliver our twins at a different hospital.

Proverbs 16:9 says, "A man's heart deviseth his way, but the LORD directeth his steps." I'm not suggesting God wanted my child to die. I chose this scripture to emphasise that we had not consulted God on the majority of the decisions we made. We were spiritually blind and unconscious, enveloped in a covenant of misery and losses.

During my eighth month of pregnancy, my son's sac burst and I slipped trying to get out of the bathtub. My father and Nate drove me to a downtown hospital because my gynaecologist was not able to come to my assistance. On top of being terrified, I experienced emotional distress because of my stay at this hospital. I was in labour, attempting to postpone the arrival of the twins at twenty-eight weeks. The hospital was in shambles, the doctors and nurses had forgotten their bedside manners, and I wasn't used to being around rude people. What a sledgehammer!

The doctor told me that his objective was to keep the pregnancy going as long as possible. He gave me medication to keep me from getting an infection because my son's sac had ruptured but still had enough fluid to support him. I was tired of being in this hospital and wanted to get out! I stayed for a few days - it felt like a week. My darling twins, Takato Altair and Atali, whose names meant "exalted" and "pure" were born on December 31, 2015, rather than March 31, 2016.

On my birthday (New Year's Eve), at 7 a.m., I gave birth to these munchkins. For the first in a long time I felt accomplished, not worthless. After birth, they were placed on the CPAP (continuous positive airway pressure) machine which assisted them in breathing, as they were born prematurely.

The doctor expressed concern about not having the necessary incubators and requested that the twins be relocated to another facility that had the necessary ventilators. Later that day, Takato had to get a blood transfusion but he died shortly after receiving the transfusion. I was terrified and in anguish. I couldn't believe I had lost him. That was the first time I ever heard Atali cry, when her brother died. She could feel it, and she knew he was no longer with her. A nurse encouraged me not to become despondent because I still had Atali and her statistics were good. Regrettably, I discovered the next day that Atali's statistics had plummeted, she wasn't doing well.

When I got released later that night, I went to visit her before I departed. I sang her a couple of songs, enthralled at her beauty. She looked like a doll with the cutest eyes imaginable, and I longed to hug her and lay her on my chest. The nurse told us she wouldn't make it and I asked if we could take her off the machine. I didn't want her to have that tube in her anymore if that was their report.

I trusted the doctor's report more than God's. I didn't even remember or cared to consult God and invite Him to break the bonds of wickedness and death that claimed the lives of my three kids. Later on that night while I was at home I received a call from the hospital to say Atali had passed. I wept bitterly.

CHAPTER 4

Open the Eyes of The Blind

I knew you in the wilderness, In the land of great drought.

Hosea 13:5 KJV

How do you put into words how you feel after losing three wonderful children? That difficult period in my life was filled with death, grief, and instability. I was very frail. I remember not wanting to get out of bed, eating little for weeks, losing weight, and living in constant discomfort, despair and terror. One night, Nate wanted to call it quits on his life and mine. He wanted to end both of our lives out of despair. I knew I had no intention of dying. I was depressed and heartbroken, not suicidal. I blamed myself, God, and the Jamaican health care system.

Nate and I grew apart over time; he wanted to push on and remain positive, and I wanted to wallow in my grief. I believed that if I immersed myself in the agony and gradually worked through my emotions,

I would heal at the appropriate moment. Nate would often comment on how depressed I was and that generated a schism because I couldn't understand why he wasn't as upset as I was. He used to complain about spending money on ultrasounds and worried about what he had to buy for me in preparation for the births. So, I assumed he was now probably thrilled that he no longer had to spend on children he previously said he didn't want. I was irritated.

I found out I was pregnant later that year, and I was terrified. I was even more frightened about what Nate would think. I wasn't sure if my heart could bear another loss, even though I had always asked God to grant me a child after everything I had been through. I even said I would in turn dedicate my child back to Him, just allow him to live.

Initially, Nate was happy when I finally told him I was expecting our fourth child and then he became unhappy and stressed. I hated that he was always stressed and worried because his negativity affected me emotionally. I felt vulnerable and helpless. My only respite from this sea of negativity was when I went out to work.

I was working as a Human Resources Administrator alongside my mother and aunt. It felt good to get out there and contribute. I enjoyed assisting others and this job confirmed that I still had that desire within me. I believe it was a gift God bestowed on me.

When my mother discovered that I was pregnant, she was both excited and concerned. My gynaecologist suggested that I get a cervical cerclage, a medical procedure where the opening of the cervix is sewn shut to prevent premature birth. As a result, I was placed on bed rest and this was exhausting and uncomfortable. I cried throughout the entire surgery, not because it was painful, I was physically numb, but because I was in emotional misery.

For some strange reason, I knew I was having a boy and this was later confirmed at my next doctor's visit. I had an ultrasound every week and Jorge grew at an incredible rate. I believed that he would be an exceptional child, a rapid learner. Nate and I opted not to tell everyone the wonderful news since we suspected that someone out there didn't want us to have our children. Thankfully, our family gathered together to pray for baby Jorge's safety.

Nate and I experienced dreams and visions concerning Jorge for months. I saw myself with Jorge inside our house, taking him from one room to the next. Nate had a vision of Jorge racing in our hallway with a bucket over his head, laughing and running. I won't lie, it felt exciting. I always returned to those visions for solace, and I wrote a lot during my pregnancy. Writing was and still is my passion and it aided my growth.

Though I wasn't a firm believer in Christ, in hindsight I saw God's helping hand in our circumstance, even if it was filthy. He was well aware of what He was doing. At thirty-five weeks I decided it was best to birth to Jorge at thirty-seven weeks instead of thirty-nine weeks. The doctor wasn't sure about it but I insisted he induce me at thirty-seven weeks.

When Jorge was born, he came out blue and I heard no sounds. I was worried and anxious, wondering why I wasn't hearing him cry and trying not to freak out. Minutes later, after a few rubs, I heard a cry and learned that he was delivered at 10:37 p.m. on March 10, 2017. I thanked God and relaxed. I was put to sleep while they extracted the rest of the suture thread from the cerclage I had in place. My son was with his father and my mother when I was awakened and taken to my room. At three o'clock in the morning, we were shown to our room. My son was finally in my arms, just as God had shown and promised.

I was overjoyed, cried happy tears, and kissed my son as quickly as I could. I was so grateful to have him in my life that I didn't want anything negative to tarnish it. God had paved the path for Jorge to enter our lives, but there were other issues that needed to be addressed spiritually. Jorge rarely slept, and when he did, he always cried out as if something had wounded or scared him. He could only sleep if I slept beside him. When he was awake, he would stare at a certain portion of the wall in our room or look carefully at something. I was always convinced that someone was present, but I couldn't see them. To be honest, I thought it was strange but intriguing.

Jorge's disturbances reminded me of when Nate would have seizures and utter strange things, pretending he didn't know who I was or where he was. When Nate tried to walk he would stumble, hit his head on the wall or stutter when he spoke. I didn't share the intricate details of the seizures with my parents but I did notify them whenever one occurred. Nate was always convinced he was sick, and always admitted to having the worst kinds of illnesses. He often thought he tasted blood or passed a lot of blood in his stool, but when he consulted a physician about it, his claims were they found nothing. He was a healthy man in their eyes. Nonetheless, he was persuaded that something else was going on.

I often told my parents about Jorge's outbursts and how he stared at the wall. One day, my father experienced it for himself when he noticed Jorge staring intently on something that he could not see. As time passed, I had recurring dreams of men entering my house. Their black car would approach the gate, open it, drive to the side, and enter the back gate to my bedroom. They'd have me sit on the ground in terror. This dream happened every night, and I had no idea what it meant. I was always particularly exhausted, but I chalked it up to all the activities my body had to endure for three years in a row. While doing laundry one day, God reminded me of Job and how he lost his family and became ill with boils. I had the impression that God was telling me at the time that he would restore to me everything that had been taken from me.

And I will restore to you the years consumed by the locust, the cankerworm, the caterpillar, and the palmerworm, my large army that I sent among you

Joel 2:25-27 KJV

I clung to that scripture because I believed the promise was meant for me.

Even after the birth of Jorge, my relationship with Nate continued to deteriorate, and the Lord revealed to me that adultery had taken root in our marriage. Nate entertained a woman who thought she was in love with him and persuaded him to go on dates and spend time with her. At the time, I spent the majority of my time at home, taking care of myself and Jorge. I eventually gathered the courage to confront his infidelity, but this was in vain, as he made no efforts to end his relationship with her. It bothered me so much that I spoke to his mother about it, expressing my hurt, pain, and disappointment, and she encouraged me to pray and fast over it. I took her advice and went on a fast while looking for prayers online to assist me in breaking whatever influence was at work in my marriage. I got obsessed with removing this woman from our lives. She wasn't the only one, but what concerned me the most was that she was the only one to whom Nate clung and expressed sentiments of love.

Nothing went as I planned, to the best of my knowledge, as they continued the illicit relationship. What I didn't grasp was that I needed to repent and acknowledge that God had given me legal grounds to plead on my husband's behalf. Nate and I suffered unnecessary pain and turmoil because Christ was not at the centre of our lives and relationship. Almost everything, except Jorge, went wrong. Life was made excessively difficult by our hardened ears and blind eyes. Our backs were turned to God, and the difficulties glared down on us. Because of our spiritual ignorance the covenant of adultery continued to have an effect on our marriage. I refused to accept his actions and regularly stated my displeasure with the situation.

The good news is that God's hand was still at work in my circumstances. He found a way to reach out to me. When the doctors advised me to take Jorge for morning walks to decrease his bilirubin levels, I began to spend more time with God whilst strengthening my relationship with my son. And when my son was asleep, I found time to write about my feelings.

Nate stubbornly clung to his extra marital affair and when an opportunity came for him to work overseas I hoped this would bring about a positive change in our relationship, however, I also had a nagging feeling that he would not return home to us. One Saturday, the only picture frame we had with a picture of us fell to the ground and split down the middle. We thought it was strange that the frame had collapsed like that but this seemed to forebode a split between us.

Nate's departure did not lead to any improvements in our relationship, in fact things became considerably worse. He got more forceful and demanding of my time, even becoming suspicious if I didn't answer my phone on time. We had frequent disagreements but I kept my frustrations under control. I didn't want to aggravate the situation so I tried to placate him by being at his beck and call at all times. One day, Nate announced that he missed his return date and consequently he would not be returning home to us. Little did we know that all of these changes needed to happen so that God could begin a new chapter in both mine and Jorge's life.

CHAPTER 5

Deliverance in Jesus 'Name

Thou shalt no more be termed forsaken; neither shall thy land any more be termed desolate: but thou shalt be called Hephzibah, and thy land Beulah: for the Lord delighteth in thee, and thy land shall be married.

Isaiah 62:4 KJV

To make himself feel better, Nate tried convincing me to take Jorge and leave Jamaica, which I thought was insane. I had already launched a business for us in order to help him with finances whenever he came home. The other reason was that I finally wanted to resume my studies, and the third was the state of our marriage. I believed our situation would have been worse if I had taken our son illegally to another country to live with him. And I knew he would still be cheating, I would have little freedom and I would still have to deal with his craziness.

I did not want to undergo that ordeal again, but I was afraid to tell him because I felt bound by dread. Finally I found the strength to inform him that I would not joining him and as expected, he was furious. To be honest, I don't think he was upset because I wouldn't come. I think he was upset because I said 'no'. As the days passed, the verbal abuse became more frequent. He even accused me of abandoning our marriage. The relationship became so toxic and overwhelming that one day I sat on a couch and implored God to take control of the problem. I was done trying to mend it and He would have to fix it.

Significantly, after I told him, "no", I felt free and unburdened. God later revealed to me that I had been under the control of an oppressive spirit, and He had released me from it. With the Holy Spirit by my side, this was the beginning of my newfound delight in the Lord. I no longer had the desire to smoke or drink and these were problems I had struggled with when I was married and pregnant. As Jesus said:

Come unto me, all ye that labour and are heavy laden, and I will give you rest. Take my yoke upon you, and learn of me; for I am meek and lowly in heart: and ye shall find rest unto your souls. For my yoke is easy, and my burden is light.

Matthew 11:28-30 KJV

I knew without a doubt that God completely healed me; I didn't cry for him, I wasn't depressed, I was free, and I liked it. This was the beginning of my deliverance.

The final steps to conclude my deliverance were set in motion through a period of intense dreams. I would have horrific dreams at night that I didn't comprehend. One of the most significant included my Grandmother who was terribly ill and in the hospital. In the dream, she came before me on her verandah and said I should take care of my family and that she loved us deeply. I told her I would. Then, my grandfather who had already passed stood across the lane from their house, saying, "Come no Lena, I am waiting on you." My Grandma responded, "I will soon come, I am not ready yet." I shared this dream only with my close family members. After that dream, my grandmother came home from the hospital. I was especially happy that she got to spend time with Jorge and gave him the blessing of the Lord.

The second significant dream also involved my Grandma. This time my grandmother told me that she was leaving, that she loved me and my family, and that she would see me again. I awoke determined to share with my parents about my dream and discovered that my grandma had died at the same time in the early hours of the morning.

I wanted to cry, and I did, but I was comforted because of the dreams I had. Through the dreams she took the time to tell me how much she loved us all and how sorry she was leaving. I'll never forget it. After she died, I started experiencing other dreams about her and two of my aunts. In one dream I saw her sleeping on a hassock with two of my aunts beside her. In another dream, we were driving down a Kingston road when a masquerading ghost talked to me in a strange language. One of aunts asked what the ghost had said and I replied, "I don't know what she's saying," and the ghost became agitated. Oftentimes, I hear people talk about how happy and comforted they feel when their loved one who passed away visits them in their dreams. I am here to enlighten you with a scripture **(Ecclesiastes 9:5)** that talks about the dead not having anything to do with the living.

For the living know that they shall die: but the dead know not anything, neither have they any more a reward; for the memory of them is forgotten

Ecclesiastes 9:5 KJV

I told one of my aunts about my recurring dreams, and she had no idea what to make of it until she met a man named Kevin L.A Ewing, who had the gift of interpreting dreams and teaching God's word. She emailed me a video he had on dreaming about the dead, and after viewing it my relationship with Christ deepened. Of course, I was dubious at first, but everything the man said made sense to me as he was able to describe some of the circumstances I had been in, both good and bad.

I told God that if His words and gift of dreaming were genuine and He wanted me to join His kingdom, He should show me His way in a way that I could receive it. God spoke to me in the language of the supernatural world, which had long piqued my interest. Kevin Ewing spoke about the laws and guidelines for spiritual living under God's protection, and these videos aided me in my deliverances. My aunt also sent me Cindy Trimm deliverance YouTube videos, and I felt the spirit of the Lord deliver me from several strongholds.

Throughout all of this, I was pursuing custody of my son, and the Lord gave me a vision. In the vision I was reaching into my mouth and pulling a lengthy stream of things from the pit of my stomach, which felt amazing. I knew in my spirit that this was God showing me my deliverance. There were a lot of things that needed to be uprooted and He took care of them. I felt the transformational power of God through deliverance, I felt and thought differently. And, the following day my court case was ruled in my favour amidst my fasting and deliverance.

Many doors began to open for myself and Jorge. He was no longer disturbed by the spirits who had haunted him at night as a young child. The spiritual door was now shut for all the thieves who used to break into my home and infiltrate my life to kill, steal, and destroy. I know now how important it is for me to pray for God's protection over my life and the lives of my loved ones. I knew, and the demons knew, that I had been spiritually awakened, thanks be to God. I was coming for them with God's wrath.

For weeks, my entire being was fired up like a furnace for God; I wanted more and more of Him. In one particular nightmare with Nate and his mistress, I couldn't speak, though I tried. I felt and saw everything that happened physically and took place in the spirit. When I shared this with someone in a Facebook group, Words of Wisdom by Minister Kevin L A Ewing, they told me I had a deaf and dumb spirit. She asked if I had read the Bible, and I informed her that I had not since I didn't feel the need to, especially because I didn't comprehend what it said. After that encounter, I began reading my Bible and sought the Lord for spiritual insight, and the Holy Spirit fed me, led me through my battle ground, and gave me an understanding of His word and the anointing that was on Minister Ewing.

CHAPTER 6

Revelations

So God created man in his own image, in the image of God created he him; male and female created he them.

Genesis 1:27 KJV

Since Adam and Eve ate the forbidden fruit, God has given us options because we now have the ability to perceive all things spiritual and physical, just like our Heavenly Father. After all, He says we were created in His image and likeness, and the true us is the spiritual entity within our bodily frame.

All of this is to demonstrate that Satan's primary objective on this globe is to gather as many souls as possible to join him in the endless lake of fire. You may wonder how he pursues us. He pursues us by luring us to breach God's rules by engaging in adultery, idolatry, fornication, lying, speaking falsely about our brothers, gossiping about them, and hating them when we should be loving them.

After I gave my life to Christ, he revealed the truth behind some of the experiences I had in my life. I relished every nugget He tossed my way. The first revelation He gave me described a wicked twisted spirit that duped people into believing they were homosexuals, a deception from the bottom of hell. The other revelations shed light on the type of music we listen to, and I felt compelled to create an article about it called, "Witchcraft in the Music Industry," that I published on Facebook for others to read.

Nate and I used to watch a fair amount of horror movies, which I grew to enjoy. I recall watching the first *Conjuring* movie and smelling a bad odour in our bedroom. I asked Nate if he smelt it, and he said 'no', which struck me as odd. Nonetheless, I kept watching it.

My last time watching a scary film happened months before I experienced my first deliverance, when I had Jorge. Nate and I opted to watch *The Nun*, and being the inquisitive person that I am, I looked into the movie's origins after it concluded. Whatever I found terrified me. I experienced a sense of terror and death, and I quickly exited the site and switched off my phone. Nate inquired what happened, and I told him what I did, and he was outraged, wondering why I would do something like that. I replied that I was intrigued. Of course, a week later, during the wee hours of the morning I was walking Jorge up and down the corridor, trying to get him to sleep. I looked in my bathroom and saw *the Nun* by my shower. I was so shocked and scared I never watched another horror movie. The Lord revealed to me what my mom and dad had repeatedly preached to us as children: we ought to be cautious of what we listen to and see. Our eyes and ears are portals for receiving both holy and evil things. We must be cautious allowing either light to enter through the Word of God or darkness to enter through the pleasures of the world.

Another thing He revealed to me was about my children who died, not because of illness, but because they were sacrificed. The devil does not play fair, and when we disobey God's commandments to gratify our desires, there is a cost to pay, whether we realise it or not.

Men do not despise a thief, if he steals too satisfy his soul when he is hungry; But if he be found, he shall restore sevenfold; He shall give all the substance of his house

Proverbs 6:30 KJV

I also know that if any one goes through with an abortion, they would have sacrificed their precious baby to the spirit of Molech. Molech is a deity whose worship is defined by the propitiatory sacrifice of children by their own parents.

It was revealed to me that Satan also wanted my living child, Jorge. In my dreams, there came a time when I was searching for my child in complete darkness. I would pray for him, knowing that he was found in the spirit and unharmed. In other nightmares, spirits would reveal to me the harm they had done. I recall a weekend Jorge and I spent with Nate's mother, and I dreamt that Jorge and I were in a burning house, and people outside were dumping liquid on us and on Jorge's face, making his eyes look odd. I awoke quickly and wanted to discuss the dream with my then-mother-in-law, but opted not to; instead, I rebuked the dream, prayed and returned to bed.

When we awoke, Jorge wanted to play with the twins who lived at the back of his grandmother's main house, so I got him ready to go. I heard Jorge crying out a few minutes later, so I rushed to him. Jorge had apparently followed one of the twins up the dresser, and the iron had fallen, but the cord had landed near Jorge's eyes. I held my child and womb while she told the story. The dream flashed through my head, along with the words, "Imagine if I didn't pray, thank you Lord."

Harken on to what the Lord says and you shall live out your days upon the land of the living in peace.

At the beginning of my transition, I realised something important. I never loved God through my early pre-teen years. I said I loved him but my actions said I was praising Satan through the music I listened to and the movies I watched. I was lustful, had anger issues and of course, told lies when necessary. My sins grew into strongholds.

I was spiritually weak and dealt with a lot of mind fog. My mind was always creating fantasies and I always took pleasure in being hurt emotionally in my fantasies. I would argue in my mind about whether or not I was going to hell. When thoughts of being condemned to hell entered my mind, I would try to reassure myself that I was good and kind and these traits could save me from hell.

I grew to understand throughout this inward conversation that it was the Holy Spirit speaking to me; and He reminded me that being good doesn't permit anyone to enter the Kingdom of God. I had to confess that I was living a wicked and sinful life. I know, it sounds harsh but I had to see the truth for what it was in order to give my burdens to God. Once I did, everything changed for good and He took me on a ride of revelations. Are you righteous?

Are you pure? Are you living in truth according to God?

He showed me the worshipping of deities and witchcraft that it is prevalent in most martial arts activities, and I think that by participating in the roda, I was paying my respects to the numerous gods that were present in the ring! Unknowingly, I practised idolatry. I sang and clapped for all the gods and goddesses they summoned with their praise chants.

God also delivered me from astrology; my parents warned me at an early age not to read the astrology parts of the newspaper, but I did it for fun. As I grew older, I turned to astrology for guidance for the days, months, and years ahead. A lot of people enjoy branding themselves to the different astrological signs they fall under and claiming all sorts of personality traits, whether good or bad. What a lot persons are yet to see is that behind each zodiac sign is an evil spirit ready to take hold of who you are. How is that done? By declaring a zodiac sign. Remember what God says in **Proverbs 18:21**, it says, "Death and life are in the power of the tongue: and they that love it shall eat the fruit thereof." Take note, God never identified us according to the stars in the sky. Why is that? Because we were made in the image of our

Heavenly Father, we are who He says we are. His thoughts are good and pure and never the opposite.

I also believed Him when He said that seizures are demonic manifestations. It made perfect sense, because every time Nate had seizures, the spirit that took over would ask questions and his face would become twisted and scary. At the end of each episode, which concluded with him falling asleep, he had no recollection of what had been said or done. A total black out.

God also revealed to me His portions versus Satan's portions, and I now understand that sickness stems from sin and oftentimes unforgiveness. It is an evil manifestation of self-hatred and unforgiveness that must be broken by the blood of Jesus Christ, who died for our sins in order for us to live eternally in peace with Him.

But he was wounded for our transgressions, he was bruised for our iniquities: the chastisement of our peace was upon him; and with his stripes we are healed.

Isaiah 53:5 KJV

CHAPTER 7

A New Name - Hephzibah

*Thou shalt no more be termed Forsaken; neither shall thy land any more be termed desolate: but thou shalt be called Hephzibah, and thy land Beulah: for the L*_{ORD} *delighteth in thee, and thy land shall be married.*

Isaiah 62:4 KJV

After hearing a podcast about a man who was given a new name, I longed for God to give me a new name. If He could do it for Abraham, Sarah, and others, He could certainly give me a new name. I offered a brief, heartfelt prayer to God, seeking a new name. In a dream at 11:00 p.m. on October 26, 2021, I saw someone standing in their kitchen with a person standing in front of them. As I looked on, I heard the Lord's voice call me Hephzibah four times.

I tried my hardest to memorise the word so that when I woke up, I could look it up on Instagram before searching for this unusual name on Google.

I couldn't find anything on Instagram save the definition from the Bible, which says, "My delight is in her." Hephzibah was a minor character in the Bible; she was King Hezekiah's wife, and God promised her a new life in Him, saying, "No longer will they call me deserted, or my land desolate. But I will be known as Hephzibah, and my land will be known as Beulah, because the Lord will take interest in me, and my land will be married." I wept! For the first time in my life, I felt sincerely rewarded for making amends in my life. It was so personal and loving. I received a new name, promises, and insight into how God perceived me. In His palm, I was forgiven and remade.

I wrote this book with YOU in mind, to share God's grace, to enlighten and encourage you to never give up on seeking God. He shared with me that we still have the power to encounter Him because we are alive. As long as we have that gift of waking up each day, we have a chance to renew our lives in Him. Don't miss out on the blessings of eternal life because you don't want to give up the worldly poisons. With the help of the Holy Spirit, demons will be cast out in Jesus' name, Yeshua Hamashiac.

Now is your time to be awakened in the realm of the spirit and to advance in His name. Amen.

I have included a list of prayers you can use
on your journey to finding your purpose in
Christ.

My Prayer For You

I pray the Lord will continue to convict you of the things that are not pleasing to Him and to displace all hurt, turmoil, and sicknesses with the riches of the Almighty God who reigns. The One who adorns our heads with diadems as we step into the overflow of the Almighty.

As you continue to embark on your walk with the Lord, you can wield Isaiah 54:17 that says "No weapon formed against me shall prosper and every tongue that rises against me shall be condemned. This is the heritage of the servants of the LORD, and their righteousness is of me, saith the LORD".

Move forward in the Lord and may His angels take charge of you and the paths He has designed for you.

Be blessed and magnified in Him.

Amen.

Prayer Against Fear

Heavenly Father,

I thank you for giving me the authority as your child to trample upon snakes and scorpions. Your word says we are to come to you in our times of need and today Lord I remind you of your word **Ephesians 6:12**, " For we wrestle not against flesh and blood, but against principalities, against powers, against the rulers of the darkness of this world, against spiritual wickedness in high places."

Today I rebuke every spirit of fear that is trying to take place in my life, I uproot every spirit of fear, hurt and unforgiveness and yield them unto you. Every cantankerous seed must be uprooted in Jesus' name because I know God hath not given me a spirit of fear but a spirit of love and sound mind in Jesus' name.

Amen.

Prayer For Breaking Soul Ties

Heavenly Father,

I confess all sins that I have committed against You. With your word and the authority You have given me as a child of the Most High I denounce and renounce every spirit of lust, sexual iniquity, and sexual perversion. I cut off all unhealthy soul ties that were established and rebuke all negative effects that seek to take root in my life and be uprooted in Jesus' name.

Amen.

Prayers For Cancelling Assignment from the Devil in a Dream

Heavenly Father,

I come to you as a child of God. I yield my heart to You and ask that you forgive me as I have forgiven myself and others in your name. I rebuke every assignment sent to throw me off the destiny you have ordained for me to live in Jesus' name. I ask Lord, that you will give me the grace and mercy to trample upon all evil assignments and to walk in the fullness of the will set out for me in this world. I curse every spirit of stagnation, infirmity, lust, unforgiveness, slothful behaviour, and mind fog in Jesus' name.

Amen

Prayer Against The Spirit Of Oppression

Heavenly Father,

I thank you for redeeming me of all my sins by dying on the cross. I believe that you rose after the third day and ascended to Heaven to prepare a place for us, Your children. With that same faith, I thank you for taking me out of the hands of the enemy. Show me, Lord, the doors that need to be closed so the devil has no legal rights in my temple and ask that you forgive me of all the sins I have committed. With that Lord, I take up the sword of the spirit in 1 John 1:9 which says, "If we confess our sins, He is faithful and just and will forgive us our sins and purify us from all unrighteousness."

I stand in the authority of Jesus Christ and I rebuke every spirit that seeks to oppress my life in every way. I curse that oppressive spirit and send it to the pits of hell in Jesus' name. I now ask you, Father, to send your angels to encamp around me wherever I go and to minister your word to my heart. I decree healing and peace over my life on this day.

Amen

Prayer For Protection

He that dwelleth in the secret place of the most High shall abide under the shadow of the Almighty. I will say of the Lord, He is my refuge and my fortress: my God; in him will I trust.

Surely he shall deliver thee from the snare of the fowler, and from the noisome pestilence.

He shall cover thee with his feathers, and under his wings shalt thou trust: his truth shall be thy shield and buckler.

Thou shalt not be afraid for the terror by night; nor for the arrow that flieth by day;

Nor for the pestilence that walketh in darkness; nor for the destruction that wasteth at noonday.

A thousand shall fall at thy side, and ten thousand at thy right hand; but it shall not come nigh thee. Only with thine eyes shalt thou behold and see the reward of the wicked.

Because thou hast made the Lord, which is my refuge, even the most High, thy habitation; There shall no evil befall thee, neither shall any plague come nigh thy dwelling.

For he shall give his angels charge over thee, to keep thee in all thy ways. They shall bear thee up in their hands, lest thou dash thy foot against a stone.

Thou shalt tread upon the lion and adder: the young lion and the dragon shalt thou trample under feet.

Because He hath set his love upon me, therefore will I deliver him: I will set him on high, because he hath known my name.

He shall call upon me, and I will answer him: I will be with him in trouble; I will deliver him, and honour him.

With long life will I satisfy Him, and shew him my salvation.

Psalm 91 KJV

Glossary

Affliction:

1. The state of being afflicted; a state of pain, distress, or grief.

Altar:

1. A mount; a table or elevated place, on which sacrifices were anciently offered to some deity.

2. Earth or unhewn stone erected for the offering of sacrifice; in some instances, they appear to have been only memorials.

Authority:

1. Legal power, or a right to command or to act; as the authority of a prince over subjects and of parents over children.

Bloom:

1. The opening of flowers in general; flowers open or in a state of blossoming; as, the trees are clothed with bloom.

2. The state of youth, resembling that of blossoms; a state of opening manhood, life, beauty, and vigor; a state of health and growth, promising higher perfection; as the bloom of youth.

Bondage, Stronghold:

1. Spiritual subjection to sin and corrupt passions, or to the yoke of the ceremonial law; servile fear.

Deliverance:

1. To set free.

2. Release from captivity, slavery, oppression, or any restraint.

3. Rescue from danger or any evil.

Deserted:

1. Wholly forsaken; abandoned; left.

Desolate:

1. Solitary; without a companion; afflicted.

2. Deserted by God; deprived of comfort.

Diadem:

1. The tiara of a King.

2. Badge of royalty.

Discern:

1. To see or understand the difference; to make a distinction; as, to discern between good and evil, truth and falsehood.

2. To separate by the eye or by understanding.

Enemy:

1. The devil.

Forgiveness:

1. The act of forgiving; the pardon of an offender, by which he is considered and treated as not guilty.

2. The pardon or remission of an offense or crime.

Healing:

1. Curing; restoring to a sound state.

Hephzibah:

1. "My delight is in her."

2. The symbolic name of Zion, representing the Lord's favor toward her.

Molech:

1. An idol of the Ammonites.

2. According to Jewish tradition, the image of Molech was of brass, hollow within, situated outside Jerusalem. "His face was that of a calf, and his hands stretched forth like a man who opened his hands to receive something from his neighbor. And they kindled it with fire, and the priests took the babe and put it into the hands of Molech, and the babe gave up the ghost."

Possessed:

1. Held by lawful title; occupied; enjoyed; affected by demons or invisible agents.

2. To hold or occupy without title or ownership.

Prophecy:

1. To foretell, before, and to tell. (Note: This ought to be a written prophecy.)

2. A foretelling; prediction; a declaration of something to come.

Refuge:

1. Defense, high fort (tower).

2. That which shelters or protects from danger, distress, or calamity; a stronghold that protects by its strength; or a sanctuary that secures safety by its sacredness; any place inaccessible to an enemy.

Revelation:

1. Uncovering, a bringing to light of that which had been previously wholly hidden or only obscurely seen.

2. Divine guidance or inspiration from the Holy Spirit.

Testimony:

1. Witness or evidence.

Yeshua Hamashiach:

1. Jesus the Messiah.

ABOUT THE AUTHOR

Maaya Rodriques is a woman of God whose intent is to spread the fire of God with the talent God gave her.   Hephzibah is her first book; the Lord instructed her to write after her early yet harsh lessons which led her into God's presence. She enjoys assisting others in need and spending time with her family, the most. Her heart's desire is to continue walking the path God has laid her, to drive out unclean spirits and to leave a godly imprint on those she comes across. In her spare time, she writes thought-provoking articles for those who were lost but are now found in God.